CAUGHT UP:

Life in a jail cell

Introduction

There are many women who all get caught up in the system at some point in their life. They either learn how to deal with life in jail or sometimes they cannot cope being caged up. Some women find god, others tend to find their selves. Some die in a place they feel is a different kind of hell, while others find the one love they have been looking for all of their lives. Some of these women have been bought here for a crime they never committed. Some women never see the inside of a cell and get someone else caught up in their mess. It does not matter what the reason or circumstance or situation, all of these women will forever be a part of one another. They can and will always be able to relate to one another. In the next few pages you will hear the story of 20 different women and how the experience we all know as jail, changed their lives forever. No matter if it is good or bad, they all had something to say to someone, anyone who would be willing to take the time out and listen.

Part one

Kiki

As I look at myself in the mirror, I keep thinking in my head, why me? Why did I turn myself in? I should have kept running. But, it is too late now. I guess I have to suffer the consequences. I finish washing my hands. I head back into the room where my lawyer, the judge, and the officers sit. I sit down and I start to cry. I have a talk with my lawyer and she says that I should prepare myself for what is coming next. The officer standing to my left asks me to put my hands behind my back. I was in shock; I could not even believe it myself. All I remember, after that moment of being handcuffed, were my eyes seeing a bright fluorescent light before everything went dark when my head hit the concrete floor.

SJ

It was a cold, crisp night. I was getting off from work when I started blasting my music. I lit the rest of my blunt I had left over as I drove out the parking lot. I called my home girl to let her know I was on my way and to have one rolled when I got there. I was taking the last puff of the blunt I had rolled before I went into work. I was too amped up. It had been 10 long hours and I needed a girl's night out. As I started speeding down the street, I see flashing light in my rear view mirrors and proceed to pull over. I nearly shit on myself trying to stay calm and get rid of the weed smell seeping through the car. I pulled over and rolled the windows down. The cop came to the car and asked for my license and my registration. I handed it to him and he went back to his car. I let out a sigh of relief. I was thinking to myself that he did not smell the aroma of the granddaddy purp I was smoking. He came back to the car and asked me to step out and put my hands behind my back. I got out wondering what happened, how I ended up out of my car, and in these hand cuffs. The cop then put me into the back seat of his car. As I sat in the back of the cop car trying to ask the cop why I was being arrested, he yelled at me to shut the fuck up. I do not exactly remember why I made the next move I did, but oh well. I do remember seeing red. Not red from the flashing lights on the cop car that was now pulling into the parking lot. It was red from anger that I felt within myself. I may have been mad but I do know that cop was pissed. Well at lest he looked like he was when he noticed my boots going through the back driver side window.

Robyn

I was so ready for the day. They finally got his ass. I sit and I start to think about how I had 2 more kids with my baby daddy, even after he left me with the first one to raise on my own. I was so stupid for my baby daddy. It was more than sad. The joke was on him this time though. He will finally have to pay me what I am due. He will have to pay all the back child support for all these kids. I am sitting in the courtroom and waiting to be called by the judge when, I cannot help but think, maybe I should have let the kids go to school today. I then think, maybe me bringing them will give me a little bit of leverage. Either way, his ass is going down. I look around the court room and notice a woman on her cell phone sitting two spaces away from me. I see an officer coming towards us so I tap the woman on her shoulder to let her know but, she jerks away and yells at me not to touch her. Before I can catch myself, I yell back, "Well fuck you too." Before I know it, the officer is walking up to us and asks us both to leave out of the court room. I tell my mother, who is there with me, to hold the baby as I get up and leave out the room. I try and explain to the woman, as we are walking out, why I touched her as calmly as I could. She was so mad that she was yelling and cursing. My calm went to anger real quick. Next thing I know, fists were being thrown and she and I were being broken up by police officers. As fast as they broke us up, is as fast as it took them to hand cuff us. We both ended up in cuffs and sitting in a room waiting to be detained and finger printed. All I could think about at that moment were my kids, who were in the custody of my dead beat ass baby daddy.

Lizzie

There is nothing like giving someone all of you, just for them to send you to jail. I had been with my girlfriend for over 10 years. The night of our anniversary, also the night I planned to propose, everything went wrong. I am sitting here in hand cuffs in the back of the cop car wondering where things went wrong. Just 5 hours ago I was texting her saying that I had a surprise waiting for her at home. And 3 hours ago, I called to tell her to get dressed. I made reservations at her favorite restaurant, which we were supposed to be at 2 hours ago. Now, here it is, 3 hours later and I am being charged with domestic violence. It was all because I hit her, when she threw a pair of scissors and a monkey wrench at me. I mean yeah, I would take my charge for hitting her, but it was all in self defense. Had she not went through my old cell phone, and found text messages from 2 years ago when we split up, none of this would be going on. Damn that cell phone! I should have thrown it away or sold it weeks ago, like I planned to do. If I would have known this would happen, I would have never changed my number to please that dumb hoe in the first place. I would have kept the damn phone and just left her ass a long time ago.

Becky

I know that I maybe a tad bit insane, but only for the people I love. When my mother got sick I thought I was going to die. The last day I saw my mother, not only did she take her last breath, but that was the day I came to this place; I now wear a jacket that makes me hug myself 23 hours out of the day. But, it was not my fault. When the ambulance, I had to wait 1 and ½ hours for, showed up at my house I was pissed. I wanted to get my mother to the hospital. It took them a good 20 minutes to check my mother's vitals, figure out what was wrong, and to load her into the ambulance. So instead of waiting on them to finish talking to each other outside of the ambulance, I jumped in the driver seat, started that thing up, and took off. Off to the hospital I went. Too bad I did not have my license to drive, or maybe I would not have been taken off to jail that day like some common criminal. I am really not sure. Maybe I should ask my lawyer the next time he comes, dressed in his white suit to give me the little red pills and cup of water, if me not having my license had anything to do with my arrest that day.

Hollie

I was so tired and even more sick. It was even hard for me to keep my eyes open. My baby was crying non-stop and I just wanted her to sleep, at least for a little while. My husband was working overnight again, so I was on baby duty by myself. Being a new mom, sick with a cold, was the worst thing I could have ever experienced. It felt like every 5 minutes my baby was up wanting to either eat or get her diaper changed. I was somewhere between taking my medicine and fixing her bottle, before I realized, I had been sleep for hours and she had never woke up. I touched her and she was not breathing. I looked over at the night stand at my medicine bottle and her baby bottle; I realized I had poured my medicine into her bottle by accident. I got up in a panic and all I could think to do was call 911. The tears built up in the wells of my eyes as I tried to get the words out of my mouth when someone answered the call, "My baby is not breathing!" They sent an ambulance to my house immediately. As I rode with my daughter to the hospital, I called my husband. I was such an emotional wreck. I could not explain what happened to him over the phone. I told him to meet me at the hospital asap! Once I got to the hospital, they rushed my baby to the back into the ER. A nurse contacted my husband for me. I waited as patiently as I could. My nerves were so bad: my hands, feet, legs, everything was shaking. My husband ran through the double doors and up to me. He was trying to get me to explain exactly what happened. At the same time I was trying to get the words out to tell my husband what happened, the doctor was coming into the waiting room. As he walked up to us, all I could think was the worse, my baby was dead. I never imagined what I was about to hear next. My baby was fine, but she was in NICU. She was revived in the ambulance. She was under observation. Me on the other hand, I was greeted by two police officers. They hand cuffed and put in the back of a cop car.

Anita

When you are a child you think the world of your parents. They are like your super heroes. Your mom is super woman. She fixes all your meals, kisses all you bobos, and makes them better. She even knows the right thing to say when your first boyfriend breaks your heart. Your dad is like superman. There is no mountain too high or river to wide for him to put a smile on your face at just the right moment. He makes you feel like the true daddy's girl you are; all while, showing you how a man should truly love a woman. At least that is what I thought. But in my life, especially with how things turned out for me, I learned a little differently. I learned that parents are just people. They abandon you; they leave you stranded; they make you fend for yourself. So when I was put into a home with a set of strangers at the age of nine who beat, raped, and belittled me; I learned just how parents can become your worst enemies. Maybe it was the blood stains on the sheets that they will never find. Maybe it is the chainsaw that is missing. Maybe it is even my foster brother, who went through the same thing I did, but is still so persistent on finding his birth parents. Or maybe just maybe it is the body parts of my foster parents that they cannot seem to find. Nah, the fact that I am the prime suspect in their missing person's case, is making me have these thoughts right now.

Kate

I finally did it. I left his ass. After 30 years and two kids, I was able to say goodbye. My son and daughter are grown now, so the separation of their father and I was no surprise or shocker to either of them. I was close with my kids and told them everything. Well almost everything. They knew how miserable I was with their father. They knew it was time for me to leave and be happy, for once in my life. Now do not get me wrong, my kids were my world. They were the one thing in my marriage I did right. They were my one true happiness. But their father, he was a horrid man. He wanted a trophy wife, not a companion. I left him: the house, the cars, the land, the money and all the expensive furnishings of our life together. But then, was there a call on my cell phone from my parole officer. I went into his office as I had done for the past 20 years. He said I needed to take a drug test. In shock at his request, I immediately told him I would fail the test. He then told me that the last 5 years of my parole would be spent in jail if I was not clean. My life was horrible. I was in a house with a man I was no longer in love with. Which is the reason, I went back to smoking marijuana on a regular basis. I knew my son of a bitch ass; soon to be ex-husband was behind this. Obviously he forgot why I was on parole to begin with. I guess, I would have to remind him then.

Bow (Rainbow)

My real name is sort of unique to many people. My parents, total stoners, and bonafied hippies, may have been high when I was being born. I think they saw a rainbow after I had came from out of my mother's womb, when they named me. That is what I can vaguely remember my father telling me once when I was little, before they both passed away. But, to my pimp, that was not a name that suited me. He called me, Bow, for short. Not because Rainbow was too long or anything. It was because I was the first woman he met who could tie anything into a bow, with her tongue alone. At first, I found it kind of annoying but it soon grew on me. Well, he beat me until it did anyway. It was not until I found myself standing over his half dead body, I realized I did not like the name Bow one bit. He had taken my identity. He had taken my spirit; he had taken the sparkle inside of me along with everything else. Shit he had even taken my virginity at 16. Then, he took my first child at 17. Only, to then give me my second child, and first son, at 18. And now seven years later, he thought he would take my son's manhood. He thought I would be okay with it? NEVER! Not while I was living. Not while I was on this earth and carried a nine millimeter on me for protection. "My name is Rainbow dammit and don't ever call me Bow again. Oh, I forgot you will not be calling anyone ever again, you are definitely dead now."

Chanie

No woman should ever have to be in jail. Let alone, be in jail pregnant. At least, that is how I felt at the moment. No child should have to be bought into the world in a jail house. No one deserves that. Neither a child nor a mother should be put through this kind of stress. I could see if I had killed the woman they say I murdered in cold blood. I would feel better if there was more evidence that put me at the crime scene. Shit even if they could place me in the same state, hell even in the same damn country. But seeing how I was actually working and volunteering in another country at the time of the murder, I think that is going to be a hard task. Or at least, I thought, it would be a hard task. Then, my lawyer came to tell me my DNA was found at the crime scene. Now in a disturbed and enraged state, all I want is me and my baby's freedom. I always want my identical twin sister's ass found as soon as possible! She may have killed someone before, and I kept that secret with her. My sister is closer to me than anyone else I have ever known. We shared my mother's belly for 9 moth months for god's sake. But not this time, that poor woman was innocent and got killed for no reason, I can only assume. But, I will not risk my life to save hers. Not this time. I am no longer my sister's keeper!

Tammy

Life is such a crazy thing. One minute you are out with friends having dinner and drinking wine. Then the next minute, you are in a holding cell. You are trying to figure out why a room full of strangers, are sharing a cell. One minute you are drunk and trying to look for your set of keys hiding somewhere in your purse. The next minute you are waking up in a cop car with blood all over your shirt, pants, hands, and fingers. You are feeling the blood dripping. You are a tad dizzy, from a gash in your forehead, from the impact of hitting your head on the driver side car window. One minute you are saying, "Oh no you guys I am okay to drive myself home." The next minute, you are trying to figure out, why an ambulance is taking one person to the hospital on a stretcher and a corner is taking 2 body bags away to the morgue. Life seems to be really crazy like that.

Canella

Being raised in a small torn down city, in one of the worst places on earth, does have its disadvantages. You see so much killing and violence. You see people you love killed right before your very own eyes. You even see women selling themselves and their kids just to make a living. I must say it can take a toll on you. It will also teach you so much. It teaches you to be tough. It helps you to stand your own ground and stand up for yourself.

But then, it could also show you a side of yourself you never knew existed. For me though, it taught me how to be thrifty. It taught me how to be swift. It also taught me how to pretend to be 88 different people in 17 different states. I guess, that is why I am going to more than likely, spend my 63rd birthday in jail. Hell, I have already spent the last 36 birthdays in jail in over 10 different jails anyway. Plus, I have about seven more different jails to go. Eventually, I will get to stop having birthdays before I see those next seven jails. Well, I just keep praying to God, the birthdays come to an end and I can let him deal with me instead of the justice system. I am tired of spending birthdays in a place I am ready to leave. I hope that my maker can stop all the pain and agony and let me go home to glory really soon. My birthdays are no longer keeping me happy anymore. Especially since my body seems to be giving up on me now.

<u>Teena</u>

My father would always say that his one goal and job in life was to keep his son's out of jail and to keep his daughters off of the stripper pole. Little did either of us know, his daughter would be the one to end up in jail! Especially, since I had just turned 16 years old, and I was being charged as an adult in a murder trial. We definitely did not think that the people who filed charges against me would be my dad's co-workers and our neighbors; the same people I had been babysitting for since I was 11. I do not know if it was that I disobeyed orders and had company come over, which was my boyfriend. Maybe it was the fact that I forgot to press the button to make the pool cover activate and cover up the pool in the back yard. But I am pretty sure, because both their daughter and son, 7 year old twins, had drown; was the reason things in my life had turned far too real. It was way too real for my 16 year old self to wrap my head around. My world was starting and ending all at the same time. I had absolutely no control over any of it at all.

Layla

It is nothing like taking a puff of a nice blunt early in the morning, especially before your first class of the day. Well, that is until your day changes and you find yourself questioning people you have known all of your life. Like, how could your best friend just throw you under the bus over something so small like weed? I mean are you or are you not supposed to hold each other down and have each other's back? Maybe I am being naïve or even stupid. But if you: go to buy weed, your best friend of 10 plus years pulls out a gun on the weed man, shoots him, and takes off; I do not think you leave them at the scene of the crime to get caught? Well maybe....no I am sorry... obviously I am wrong. Clearly that is something that some people do. But, all I could do once I heard those 3 shots was duck and then run for my life. Well, that is once I came back into reality. I had enough time to realize that my best friend had jumped in the car and left me high and dry. Literally and figuratively. Once I made it back to campus, I was thinking I needed to get in my own car and drive that 1 and ½ hours until I made it back home. But by the time I had a bag packed, was about to grab my keys and walk out, the door to my dorm room was knocked down by a slew of cops. Shit! That was all I could think. I am going to kill Khloe!

Khloe

The rush you get from pulling the trigger of a gun is like no other. This is something my older brother and father and grandfather taught me far too well, at a young age on our hunting trips. But, I was no longer hunting deer. And, I was not a little girl anymore either. But, I was not trying to be a killer. How was I supposed to know when I showed up to my dealer's house he would try to stiff me for the last time; and I would have to pull out my gun I carry, for protection, and draw down on him? I mean I never meant to shoot him 3 times in the chest. I did not know for sure but, I was pretty damn positive, he was dead. But I got the worse, yet best news, was when I got back to campus. I saw a shit load of cop cars, ironically, taking Layla away in hand cuffs. I know, that was not right, what I did. Leaving her there was the hardest decision I ever had to make. She was shell shocked when she: walked in, saw me pull the trigger, and heard the shots being fired. First, I did not expect her to get out the car. I guess she wanted to buy some weed of her own. Second, when she heard the gun shots she froze up like a Popsicle. Third, all I remember thinking, I needed to get out of there. I did. But now that the cops had Layla I could go back home and see what my parents thought I should do. I mean my dad is a lawyer and my grandfather is a judge. If anyone can get me out of this mess, it would be the both of them. I plan to be a lawyer just like my dad one day so this murder cannot be on me. But my family will know what I should do. Not to mention, this 1 and ½ hour drive can give me a pretty good alibi.

Cash

Lord knows I love my girlfriend. She is everything to me, all I have. When I had no one, I had her. When I did my time in jail for possession of cocaine: when I almost got a life sentence: when she had to take one of my charges so I would not be a third time convicted felon. She was always there for me. If I cannot count on anyone else in the world I know I can count on my baby. I can always count on my little glimmer of Hope. So this time when my lawyer comes to see me, and tells me some more bullshit like, "Oh the DA wants to make a deal with you," I can say "Fuck No! Snitches get stitches." I know that my girl could never and would never turn on me. We have a bond like no other. We are damn near the same person. Shit ever our periods come down at the same time. We are that in sync with one another.

Hope

Lord knows I love my girlfriend. I really have become her everything, and her mine. When she had no one, I was there. Whenever she went to jail I held her down. She damn near got sentenced to jail for life and I was still there. Shit I even took a charge to keep her ass out of jail for a long time. But, she was working so hard at the time. I knew she would hold me down. She took good care of me while I was locked up, at least. She knows she can count on me; I am all she has. I hope she does not turn on me like I keep hearing. Especially, since her favorite line always has been that 'snitches get stitches.' My lawyer says she may make a deal with the DA and snitch on me. I am not too sure at this moment. I mean she is the yen to my yang. We even share a damn period, unfortunately. We are so in sync we are damn near the same person. I pray that she keeps the faith and knows that I am still her little glimmer of hope.

<u>Byrd</u>

I have stolen many things in my day. Money, clothes, shoes, checks, shit I even stole a house boat this one time, long ago. But this last time....and I do mean last time, stealing, definitely had to be the worst time. I was finally ready to start my life anew. I planned to steal a car, drive to the coast, hop on a boat, and sail somewhere far, far away. Well I was on my way, so I thought. I had jumped into this real nice car. The engine was on, it was all too perfect. I should have known it was too good to be true. This lady had gotten out to go inside, for what was more than likely, supposed to be a quick second to the ATM. But, I got into her car and pulled off without her even noticing me. It was not until I was about 30 miles outside of the city limits I realized she had a baby in the back of the car. I do not know if I was too eager or just that blind. Damn, how could I miss a whole baby and car seat in the back of the car? I had decided, once I got to the next exit with a hospital, I would take the baby and leave it there. I would tell them how and where to find the baby's mother. But, as fast as the plan popped into my head, the cop lights were flashing. One cop car was in front of me and two more cop cars were behind me. There was a helicopter over my head and I am pretty sure I was on the news during what now seemed to be a chase. Oh well, so much for my get away and starting anew. But, there was still something new....new charges to my rap sheet.

Lillie

Growing up with a biracial couple as parents gave me a very interesting childhood. Not only did I get the better of two different cultures, I got the worse of it as well. Do not get me wrong, not everything was so bad. I got to take from my Asian mother the value of running a successful business. And from my African-American father, I learned the meaning of the word hustle. Even though, he would try to keep the world on the streets away from me, he could not keep all my cousins from showing me certain things. So the day I got 17 stitches and had to be rushed to the hospital because of a cop, who bombarded into my nail salon trying to take down the meth lab I had been operating in the back for over a decade, I knew it was on. You see when you are used to making fast money and money fast it is very hard to stop. Yet and still, you tend to have certain things and people at your disposal. Things such as, a good lawyer with a team of bad ass people to help back him. Plus, a few friends, that work for the DAs office. Shit, you even get you some judges who sit on the bench that owe you a few favors. Not to mention, you keep a shit load of legal tender to make a lot of our problems go away. I mean yeah, I may have a metal plate being put in my head because of the cop who beat the shit out of me. But, let's just see who will get the last laugh. Let's see who will be the one in jail, and who will be the one getting out, while suing the shit out of the whole department she works for. Let's see who gets dealt the better hand. Like I said, my mother showed me how to be successful and my father showed me how to hustle.

Leslie

In my line of work, anything goes. You set your own rules. People play by your terms. You even decide who wins the game. You are not dealt a hand, you do the dealing. Now, I may not be the best at what I do, but I do a damn good job. And at one time, I even believed in doing my job the right way. I mean I took an oath. I made a promise to people. I took my job and badge as an honor. What happened between then and now, I had no idea. All I know, I am on the streets brining in the bad guys; I am not trying to be one of the bad guys. I have taken a lot of men and women to jail, but never did I ever think my own partner would turn on me, and be the reason I ended up in a jail cell. It was all over a woman, I never intended to beat on. But, when you have a perp who tries to rat on you, resists arrest, and tries to run when you bust in on them and their meth lab, things turn bad pretty fast. Now I am inside a jail, on a pod, where I have taken in a few of these women. It is so crazy to be on the inside looking out. Especially when most of these women want to kill me, I just hope that every night when I lay down to close my eyes and go to bed, I wake up in the morning. Shit, I will not lie, I want to wake up or at least not wake up dead.

Part Two

Kiki

I came back into it. The first thing I see is a huge fluorescent light. I shake my head and I think I am still on the floor. Then, I look to my left and notice a row of what looks to be hospital beds. I realize I am in the infirmary. A cop comes into the room to check on me and make sure I am up. The nurse, who is with her, gives me some pills and a little cup of water. She instructs me to take them. The cop asks me to lift up my tongue to be sure that I have taken the medicine. Then, the cop hand cuffs me. I am taken into a large room with other women. They are all spread out among 11 sets of bunk beds. I am not in the holding cell long; they finger print me and take my picture. A little while later I am hand cuffed and taken upstairs with three other women. Once I get to my own cell I start to contemplate turning myself in. I wrote a few bad checks. I stole some money. The real big reason I was here though, was because I had gotten involved in a scam with my ex boyfriend. He would get a friend to get checks from their job, a place that did taxes, and he would then print out fake amounts and get random people to cash them for a small fee. It worked out until a shit load of those people got caught and gave up my ex, in exchange for a lesser sentence. The cops came looking for us both. That was when I decided I had to disappear for a little while. Everything was fine because I had managed to set up an account and put some money on the side, just in case. It was not until I went back home, a few years later, I chose to turn myself in. What kind of dummy was I? Now I am in a cell waiting to go to court and have this pompous ass judge tell me how much time he is going to sentence me.

SJ

I am pretty damn mad I had to walk into the jail house with no shoes on my feet. I mean okay, yeah I did kick the window out of that cop's car. But come on! To let me walk in bare foot, really though? Plus there was about 10 guards waiting on little ole me like I was oh so dangerous. I am only 5'1". The cop that pulled me over was most definitely a big ole pussy, as most cops are. But it was not until I was: finger printed, photographed, and then, the moment when I and 3 other women were taken upstairs to be locked up with the rest of general population, I thought that maybe assault on an officer was not such a good charge. I mean that was really the first time that I actually sat and thought about it for a second. Maybe my temper and my anger issues do need to be put in check. Maybe I do need to start taking my meds again. Shit I may even need to talk to someone. But I definitely do not need to kick out any more got damn windows.

Robyn

When I got in the back of the cop car I knew that stupid mistake was going to cost me
big time. I had so much that was going on and nothing I could do about it. Though, I
should have been happy and I should have been grateful for my baby daddy, at that
moment, I really was not. All I could do was sit in the holding cell and wait for the next
roll call so I could find out my bond. I would then leave and go get my babies from
where ever it was my baby daddy had them. I really did hate the fact their dad had to take
them, when the cop hand cuffed me and the other lady, and sent us here. I could have
fallen to my death when I called my mother and she told me the judge gave my baby
daddy temporary custody of our kids. He also gave him an extension to pay back the child
support he owed me, since he had the children for the time being. I was relieved when I
heard the guard come through the door and finally yell, "Roll call." I heard her call out
my name. She asked me to verify my birth date, asked when I got in, and if I knew my
charges. I proceeded to tell her the information she asked for. I told her I was not sure
what I was being charged for and if I had a bond set yet. She told me my charges and
what my bond was. Good thing I am a person who always plans for the worse. If not, I
would have never been able to get my mother to go to my house and get the money I
needed to bond out. Plus, find a bail bonds with the lowest price to get me out in the
shortest amount of time possible. Once everything was done, I heard my named called,
and I was out; then and only then, would I feel better. But, it would only be a matter of
time. I will probably roll on up out of here in the middle of the night like most people
tend to do.

Lizzie

I felt like there were so many people in the holding cell with me. It was crowded by the time I got in. There were only a few empty beds, like two honestly. It was not until the deputy doing roll call that night said my bond out loud, and I was sent upstairs, that I realized my girlfriend and I were over. Do not get me wrong, we got into fights before but not to the point where she pressed charges. I was so mad I do not think I realized how much of an asshole it turned me into in the matter of minutes. I mean as soon as I got processed, took the picture they put on your wrist band, and got into my cell upstairs, I went into a rage. I started an argument with my Bunkie and that escalated farther than I had ever expected. They actually had to move me to another dorm or pod or whatever it is theses officers call it. Instead of going to another cell right then and there, I had to stay on second floor holding. That was even worse than the holding tank. I felt like I was punished from the rest of the jail since I was standing up in a tiny cell by myself for hours. Moving me did not work too well. I assume that being locked on second floor holding just made the rage I had even worse. When I got out the guard who was bringing me back was being a dick so, that turned into a huge fight with him. I never meant for things to get that bad, nor did I mean to end up in isolation either. But, I guess beating up on your girlfriend is one thing but beating up on a police officer, until he can no longer breathe, is a totally different thing.

Becky

My lawyer who wears the white suits and gives me the little red pills is an idiot. But then again, so is my lawyer who wears the fancy suits with the nice ties. Whenever I get to leave the home and go with him, we go to this big building. He takes me to this man who sits up high and looks down on us. The man must be pretty angry most of the time because; he is always banging this hammer and telling people to be quiet. He must have OCD because; he really likes the word order and always wants it in his room. He is not such a nice man though. He has made me go to this place where I do not get my own room. I have to sleep on a bunk bed and they never turn the lights off. I really hate it in here. The entire room of woman I am in the room with all got a different story of why the mean man or the police bought them here. The women keep saying I am lucky because, I get to go upstairs. But I do not feel lucky. I hear that upstairs is so much different from this place, the holding tank, they call it. I cannot lie though, I am definitely glad that when I get upstairs I get to go in a room where I can finally sleep because they do turn the lights off down here. I do not think I could go 90 days in this place with the lights on. The only good part about being here is this cool bracelet they gave me. It has a really nice picture of me. Maybe the best picture I have taken in a few months now.

Hollie

I am sitting in this cell and all I can think is I want to go home. I want this tragedy to not have happened. But, my thoughts are interrupted when the guard calls my name and two other women's names to be taken to another part of the jail house. As they shackle me to one of the women, who looked more like a girl who should have been in college, my stomach turned upside down and inside out. I kept thinking about the half a million dollar bond set for me. I was devastated. That was not the worst part of all of this, though. When I called my husband to see about getting a lawyer to represent me, hearing the hurt and pain in voice, he said I should not have the right to raise our child is what did it for me. Hearing him say he wanted a divorce did not even register in my brain until later on as I lay in my cell bed. The guard had finger printed, photographed, and sent us all upstairs to general population by now. I was not even bothered by it honestly. I could not bear the thought of not being able to see or touch or hear or even smell the scent of my baby girl. The most horrible part of it all had not even started yet. I still had to get and wait for a lawyer to see if I could even beat the charges of child endangerment set against me. I still had a long way to go.

Anita

I sat down under a spot light for long enough, so I thought to myself. I wish I could go home already. I am done with being investigated by police. My foster brother was so dead set that I had killed his parents, my foster parents. That made me fed up with this whole investigation. The cops made me come in for questioning, like I was the person who killed them. Now I know the truth, but none of them do, especially not my foster brother. All he knows is that he came to visit them on Friday afternoon and they were doing okay. Saturday morning, when he went back to the house, they were gone. Sunday night, when he went back to the house to check and see if they were there, they had not came back. Now, I may not get along with my foster brother or my foster parents, but as far as him and the police are concerned I had nothing to do with them disappearing. I mean yes, I had to come back into town for a few days to check up on them like I would normally do when I go on vacation, but that was all. Once I saw them Friday morning, I left for my vacation to this camp site that I visit about 2 hours away from their home every year. I know that after this investigation is over my foster brother is going to feel like a complete ass. They have checked my car and found no traces of blood or any types of evidence. They checked with the park rangers and my alibi is tight and right. Not to mention, the neighbors saw me come and go from my parent's house hours before my brother had even made it there. The cops have said it and he still will not believe it, but I had nothing to do with this. If anything, he was the last person to see them. Maybe he was the one who killed them. Maybe telling the cops that and possibly trying to press charges against him will get a different kind of response out of him.

Kate

I finally got to see my kids. Like I said before, they are really my happiness. My son is so
mad at his father. All he could do our whole visit was talk about getting him back for
putting me in jail. Now I know my son means well, but his dad is not to blame. I had to
let my kids know once and for all, exactly why I was still on parole. Even thought I tell
my kids almost everything, I do have a few secrets. I do know that I wanted to divorce
their father and go be happy, but I had wanted that for a long time. There was a time
though, when he meant the world to me. But, that was the time when he decided to love
me, even after killing his own flesh and blood. See what my kids do not know, their father
came from a family that was the wrong kind of wealthy. His mother had been dead since
he was born so it was just him and his dad. His dad however, controlled everything their
father did, right down to the relationships he had. So to their grandfather, bringing me
home was a big no, no. It was so big that he tried to rape me. So I drove an ice pick
through his heart. Now their father, instead of sending me to jail, he did not testify
against me. He helped me instead. For that reason, I was forever in debt to my husband.
But not anymore, I needed to be happy. I needed to get over the other things in our
horrible past and be happy for myself.

Rainbow (Bow)

I stood over the body of my pimp for another 2.5 seconds. I got my son, all his things, and sent him next door to my neighbor and best friend. She knew exactly what happened even without me telling her. She knew what to do. We talked about this day for a long time. I am not sure if you can call it premeditated or not, but it sure was murder. But, that was the last time me or my son would be a victim. I knew the cops were on their way to come take me away. I kissed my son on the forehead, hugged my best friend, and headed back home. I sat on the last step of my porch. I pulled out my lighter and a pack of cigarettes and started smoking. By the time I was almost done with my cigarette, I saw the flashing lights. I told the cops exactly what happened, everything. They cuff me and took me away in the cop car. I was only in the holding tank for a few hours before I was finger printed, had my picture taken, hand cuffed again and taken upstairs. I know that I did what was right. I know I had to stand up for me and my child. I am not worried. I can and will fight and beat this charge. He raped my son. He took the little innocence he had left. So I took his life. All is even now.

Chanie

I jumped up from my sleep. I swear I feel like I have to pee every 3 minutes. This little, not so little baby inside of me is making me go crazy. Well that, and the fact that I cannot get out of jail. If my lawyer does not find either: my twin sister, my passport, or my plane ticket stubs soon; I am going to have a break down. My twin has pulled a lot of crazy ass stunts in her day, but this by far is the craziest, even for her. I am really starting to think, no I know, that giving her access to my house and car and life was the wrong thing to do. It was a mistake, especially since I was gone out of the country for months. I do not know why I always allow her to come back into my life every time she messes up. I cut her off then I feel bad. Well, she usually makes me feel bad for exiling her from my life and I give in. I always let her back in once more. Not this time. Not after this. I am pregnant and in jail because of her. This is the last damn straw for me. My lawyer better find her. If I have to deliver my first child in jail or have to do time because of something I did not do, that I know for a fact that my sister did, then it is on. She will not have to worry about when I get out of jail. I will certainly go from being an identical twin to being my parent's only child.

Tammy

I must have sat in the holding tank forever. I felt like I saw a million people come in and leave out. I am not sure if they were going home or going upstairs; either way, they were leaving out. Plus, every time there was a roll call and my charges and bond were read, '3 counts of vehicular homicide,' I heard the light murmurs of judgment. But, when the rest of the inmates heard that there was a million dollar bond on each charge, the room fell silent. I guess a 3 million dollar bond was a bit too much for them. Oh well, is what I thought to myself. I felt bad enough. I know that I should not have gotten behind the wheel. I know I should have taken a taxi home that night. I know that I should have been the one to die in the car that night and not that family. But, things happen and I was here now. I knew I was going to be here for a while. I cannot lie, when they called my name so I could get my photo taken before I had to go upstairs, I had never been so happy. I was finally sober, and all I wanted was a nice hot shower. I wanted a nice long rest without the blinding lights that stay on 24/7 in the holding tank. I also wanted the comfort of being in my own thoughts, even if just for a second when my one roommate was sleep; instead, of the 17 or 18 people who may or may not sleep, that I shared this huge ass room with. I just needed a moment to try and at least remember what happened that night. I need to remember so I could recall the events of that night. I also need to remember so I could tell my lawyer what happened that night as well. If only I was not that drunk. Maybe, I could have a shot at another chance to finish living my life. I guess that is over at this point.

Canella

After being 88 different people in 15 years, you tend to forget who the real you is. I find myself constantly thinking back on how I have been in 10 different jails in the past 36 years. My, how time flies or drags along, when you literally have nowhere to go. Now, I am at jail number 11 in another state and I still have 6 more states to go. This would make any other person in the world go crazy but not me, not anymore anyway. At first I was scared and nervous but I let that go. Fear is not something I could hold onto. Not in jail, especially not living in the free world. But I am a fighter; I always have been, even since I was little. I came here to the states when I was only 8. My parents were poor, so I mostly stole to help us get by. I learned how easy it was to steal things at an early age. But by the time I turned 12, I found out how easy it was to steal a person's identity. And by the time I had my 21st birthday, I was a pro. It was not until I was 27 years old, I got caught. But then, I was so far deep into my scam and I had stolen so much that the death penalty was not enough for the prosecutors. So now, I get a trial in every state that I have stolen someone's identity; I do my time; then, move to the next state and start the process all over again. I wish they could have run all my time concurrent so I could get this over with in one jail. I hate moving all over the place to different jail houses. But, by the time I hit the 3rd state, I was used to it. It was not until 3 years ago, when a doctor told me I had cancer, that I gave it all to God. I mean yea, I am worried, but hell what is the worse that could happen? I die in jail? Shit that is inevitable at this point in my life. I spoke with my lawyer and he said he wants to try and get the rest of my charges thrown out because of my condition. He says that an elderly cancer patient should not have to be put through this judicial process in 6 more states. I am not saying he is right or wrong about that; all I am saying is that at least in here I get my treatment. If I go out there in the free world though, things may change. I hate to admit it, but that is where I think I would get scared.

Teena

When my mother and father walked to my neighbor's house and saw that I was hand cuffed, all they could do was wonder. They did not know what had happened and why I was in need of their help. I kept replaying the reactions on their faces from that horrible night in my head. As I sit here on the end of my bunk and think about exactly how many years I will be sentenced to, my name is called for visitation. I thought my parents were here and were coming to, yet again; make me feel worse than I already did. To my surprise, it was my boyfriend. I got into the visitation room and before I could stop myself, I burst out into tears. My head and heart were hurting. I do not know what to do or say. I just know that he looks awesome. We pick up the telephone receivers and what I think is going to be a happy conversation turns into something a lot different than what I expect. My boyfriend says that he only came to let me know he will not testify on my behalf. He also wants nothing to do with me. Enraged, I hang up the phone and leave the visit immediately. When I get back into my cell I start crying harder. My mind is racing at this point. I think that I am really starting to lose it. I cannot do this anymore. I take the head scarf I have made from my bed sheet and I tie one end to my top bunkies bed. I tie the other end around my neck. I slowly start to slide off the end of my bed. My face starts to feel funny. I can feel the blood rushing to my head and all of a sudden my whole body starts to feel numb.

Layla

My lawyer came to see me once I made my way upstairs to general population. I had to tell him everything that happened. As much as I did not want to tell on my best friend, I refused to go down for a murder I did not commit. I had known Khole since we were little. To think, she could ride past as the cops put me in the back of their cop car. She was a whole hoe out here. My bond was set so high that my parents were not even able to post my bail. My lawyer said that he would make sure to have a police sent to: Khole parent's house, our dorm room, or wherever they had to so they could question and take her into custody. They ended up finding Khloe at her parent's house. But even though she was picked up, I later found out that she was able to post bail and get out that same night. Because her dad is a well known lawyer and her grandfather is a judge, she was only held for a few hours. Me on the other hand, I am on my own. My lawyer is confident in me and my case, none the less. He is more than sure that he can get me off. I hope that for the sake of my sanity, he is right about that. I cannot take another minute in this place.

Khloe

I called my dad while I was on my way home. He knew that something was wrong when he heard my voice. He said to stop talking and get home as fast as I could. When I pulled up to my parent's house, took a shower to wash off the memories in my brain and try to clear my thoughts. I heard my mom calling for me. I got out the shower, put on my clothes, and went down the stairs. As I made my way to the kitchen, I saw the cops ready to cuff me. My dad told me not to say anything until he got back to me at the jail house. My bond was high as hell, but still, my dad paid my bond and I got out. My parents were livid. My grandfather, who is a judge, could have killed me. But even though I did what I did, they still had my back. It was not until a few days later, that I was picked up again, because they had an eye witness that put me at the scene of the crime. Someone saw my car driving away. It sucks because now I have to sit in general population until the day of my trial. I am pretty sure that my best friend is not only mad, but she is looking to take me down with her. I mean it is her fault that we are locked up anyway. If only her dumb ass had stayed in the car.

<u>Cash</u>

When my lawyer came to see me today, he did and said what I expected. They wanted to make me a deal so I could give up Hope. It would never happen. She was my strong hold. What our lawyers do not know is that the hall girl was sending notes to and from Hope and me so that we could at least attempt to communicate. I was so glad that I could read and see her handwriting. I could hear her voice in every word she wrote. She told me, her lawyer told her, there were no witnesses to put us at the crime scene. They also had no evidence of us ever even robbing the convenient stores. I was so glad to know that. Now, all we have to do is sit back, calm down and wait. We would and could be out within weeks. I was relieved to know that all my thinking and praying had worked. I knew that we could make it through. I knew if we both stayed true, held one another down, then we could beat this. Looks like my glimmer of Hope came through like I always knew she would.

Hope

When my lawyer told me that the eye witness they had was a fluke, I could not wait to write Cash and tell her. Our lawyers were trying so hard to get us to rat each other out, it was now sad as hell. I was so thankful for the hall girl we had on our floor in the jail house. She was nice enough to send letters to and from Cash and I so that we could communicate with one another. I had poured my heart and soul into each letter I wrote Cash. I made sure to let my love know that all she had to do was sit tight and wait. Patience was really a virtue right now. My lawyer said that we could possibly be out of jail within a few weeks. Just like always, I had her back and she had mine. If we were to be patient, we could be back at home, or anywhere that we chose for that matter, very soon. I guess, yet again, that little glimmer of Cash's Hope was right here where it needed to be, like always.

<u>Byrd</u>

I know that my plan to get that baby to the hospital was a little farfetched. I was being chased by the cops and on the news, but at least I tried. I made it to the hospital when the cops finally got me. I did feel a little bit better about myself. At least I did the right thing after the fact. But, after hearing the story of my Bunkie, I felt bad for her. She was a beautiful woman who I had come to know and love. We shared so much of ourselves with one another. We became very close in the process. When she first got in the room with me, I felt the need to help nurse her back to health, and make sure her recovery was a good one. No woman should have to deal with the horror of having a life threatening surgery where they have to put a plate in your head. All because of a goodie goodie cop, who bashed in her skull. Though I felt sorry for her, I respect her as well. Since we had been bunkies, she has looked out for me. She has made sure I had money on my books so I could get the personal items I needed and the snacks I wanted. She had definitely been someone that I have come to depend on greatly. I hope when I get sentenced, for simple thief and kidnapping, she will continue to hold me down. I would hate to have to serve this time alone and lose her in the process. I cannot lie, it is not just her money. It is not because she is a gorgeous Asian and Black woman. But, it is the fact that she has been the only reason I have not killed myself. She is my dream woman. She has been my light in the time of darkness. She has been the one and only reason that I have not given up on myself. She has given me a reason to keep on fighting for my life, for my love, and for us.

Lillie

The lord works in mysterious ways. When I finally came out of recovery, after getting a plate put in my head, I came into a room with a wonderful woman I have grown to love with all of my heart. My bunk mate Byrd. She is a tad bit crazy and a whole lot insane, but aren't we all. She has a beautiful soul. If not for her helping nurse me back to health, I may have lost my mind. I almost died because of a dumb ass cop Leslie Gates, bashing my head in with her gun, after I saw her stealing some of the meth they were using or supposed to be using as evidence to build a case against me. Good thing for: my cousin who is the Attorney General, my friends who work in the DAs office, and my aunt, who is not only on one of my payrolls, but is also a very well respected judge. She is the same judge who is going to convict Byrd, ironically. But, little does Byrd know, I got her. Even when she does go to do her time, she will not have to worry. I will make sure there will be money on her books and on the phone. She will be going to one of the best prisons in the state. Since she has helped me become closer to God, and become myself again, I got her. Not to mention, I saw the way she helped out this couple who came in together.

When Byrd did her hall girl duties, she would send notes back and forth to them. I respect the shit out of her for that. She could have been in trouble and lost the little she did have, but she did it all for their love. I think it was the moment when she told me she found out the cop that put the metal plate in my head was in one of the dorms, and she had one of her home girls beat her ass for me, that I fell in love with her. It was then I knew I was in love. This was the beginning of something between us. I would not let our cases stand in our way of happiness. My lawyer says that I have a pretty good case against the Police Department. He says I will more than likely have all my charges dropped and win my lawsuit against them. To be honest, I really do hope so. The faster I get this behind me, the faster I can put my time and effort and money into Byrd and her case. I can work on getting her out. And once we are two free women, we can finally be together and be happy.

Leslie

I woke this morning, but a part of me wishes that I had not. I am in the hospital handcuffed to a bed, fighting for my life. This girl that is in my dorm came into my room and basically strong armed me. I think of that last drug bust when I bashed this woman's head in and sent her to the hospital. From what I hear, she has a plate in her head now. Now, here I am waiting to see if I have to get a plate put in my jaw because of this ass whipping I took. The irony of it all just makes me sick to my stomach. I think this could possibly be the work of either her, or maybe someone she knows, or maybe someone I have put in jail. Who knows really? I mean, I know what I did was wrong. I definitely did steal a lot of meth from her, even before she noticed. I was tired of being a goody-two-shoes ass cops though. I wanted to make a quick come up like I had seen others cops, who were not so good, do from time to time. I admit, I did not have to bash in her head the way I did. Shit, my partner did not have to snitch on me afterwards either. I guess that was his payback for me finding out he was on her payroll and was helping her hide the meth lab in the first place. I guess two wrongs do not make a right but, I obviously made the wrong move because I am locked up. He is still at home; free in the outside world. Internal affairs have notified me that I am fired. I still need a lawyer. The Police Department and I are being sued by the woman whose head I bashed in. This situation definitely looks more horrible for me. Because of the investigation, and the severity of the case, every woman I have ever put in this jail house is after me. I am praying they will not return me to general population once I get out of this hospital. I hope someone somewhere has mercy on my soul.

Part Three

Kiki

50 fucking years. 50 fucking years. This stupid ass judge gave me 50 fucking years. I could feel my heart drop in my pussy when I stood before the judge with my lawyer and he said that I was sentenced to 50 fucking years. When I pled guilty, the judge sentenced me to 5 years for every year I was on the run. The charges for writing the bad checks, stealing, and also the money scam were all dropped. My lawyer was really that good. But, being on the run got me the worse time possible. 50 years was the best I could get. What the fuck was I going to do? I guess serve 50 fucking years. I am so upset. I guess going upstate will not be too bad. But I know someone is going to try and take my goodies. All these women always tell me how much they want my little Spanish ass. Muy calient is what they call me in here. Lord knows I never thought that this judge would do this shit. I cannot believe it is all I keep thinking in my head. Well that, and 50 fucking years. Shit I better make sure my dumb ass does not drop the fucking soap while I am in there. I may get another 50 fucking years for killing a bitch. I am so glad I am going to a jail where I can smoke. After all of this time, I think I need a few got damn packs of cigarettes to smoke. I shake my head and think, 50 fucking years!

SJ

My mom came to visit me today. It is always a sad visit with her. Today I told her that I did not want her to keep driving those 2 hours to come to see me. I am going to be spending the next 15 years in here because I decided to kick the windows out of a cop car. The cop, who was an asshole, did deserve it. I had never been disrespected so much in my life by anyone, and I was not about to start letting the police do it. I know that I was wrong. I know that what I did was uncalled for, but he probably needed that. I bet he will never disrespect another black woman ever a fucking gain. His ass will never curse out another woman or treat her like a piece of shit. So even if I have to sit here mad, at least I got some type of justice for another woman. I really am not too much worried though. Mad yes, but worried, not so much. I have entered myself into anger management classes and I am back on my meds regularly. I am also getting my GED and I am doing any and every little thing I can to cut some of my time off. By the time it is all said and done, my 15 years can possibly be broken down to 5 years here. The classes along with my time served, I could possibly be out of jail just in time for my 30th birthday. At least I am praying to the lord for this. I am not worried; I know God has my back. I can still have a life. I can still have a chance. I can still have the option to be the best me. I know that from now on when I see a cop, I am not going to be fucking with them. I will go in the other direction.

Robyn

It had been months since I was able to tuck my kids into bed and kiss them goodnight before they went to sleep. It was nine whole months to be exact. I was definitely excited yesterday when the judge said it was okay for my babies to come back home and live with me again. It had been a horrible battle between my baby daddy and me for the past nine months. After he was granted temporary custody of our kids, he realized what I had been trying to tell him; we have some awesome ass children. He was so vindictive towards me throughout this whole process. When they took me to jail for fighting with that woman in the court room, he actually filed for sole custody of our kids and said I was an unfit mother, He also tried to get my ass put on child support after that, since he was the one who had our kids. His ass really is an idiot. I guess I did not help the situation when I went to his house late one night, to bash the windows out his car, and he so happened to see me pulling away down the street. But the thing is, my mother so happened to call my phone and I failed to succeed at that plan. Good thing I did not do it, then, I really would not have gotten my kids back. But as a parent you will honestly do any and everything for your children, especially if you are a good mother. But I had to pray and wait and be patient. My prayers were most definitely answered. Now, I have to share custody with my baby daddy; But, I get my kids back at home where they belong. His stupid ass does not have to pay child support from when he had the children, but he will be paying all the back child support from when he was not paying me anything. So, I guess I cannot complain about all of this because I got my kids home safe and sound. I am just happy they have me to tuck them in and kiss them goodnight every night.

Lizzie

The lawyer I had warned me of the magnitude of the situation I had caused for myself. When she said that I would be facing 10 years for beating on my girl, well ex-girl, I felt that was a joke compared to the life sentenced I was facing for beating and killing a cop. Once I got to prison, I could only pray. I think life plus 10 years is one of the dumbest things I had ever heard. But, here I was. Here was my life plus 10 years. I could sit and think about my life, or I could get myself and my thoughts together to deal with the life that was ahead of me in this prison. I was going to be spending a lot of time in this cell. At least I was not alone. I had an older Bunkie, an Old Italian lady named, Canella. She was nice and very sweet. She was also very sick. I could tell that she would not be here much longer. She had cancer ever since we both got here together a few years ago. She had become one of my closest friends. She taught me about God and helped me to make a great change within myself. She helped me to develop a relationship with God and become closer to him. I would always be so grateful for her. She gave me hope and helped to make my time fly by. She had such an awesome spirit. I had a great deal of respect for her. She was the only woman, I have ever known, to tell her lawyer that she wanted to stay in jail just to have a fighting chance against her disease. She was so strong and brave so I thought. I can never forget that morning when I woke up for our daily prayer; I found her cold body and she was not breathing. I was so devastated. I hugged her one last time, covered her body, and prayed over her. I knew that she was no longer in pain now. She was no longer suffering. Like she would always laugh and say, she was gone on home to glory. I, myself was happy and sad at the same time.

Becky

It has been a fun time in this place. I am kind of upset that it has been 30 days longer than the 90 days I had to stay here. On the upside, I guess I cannot really complain. I have met some really nice women in here. I have had fun with them. I have learned to play a bunch of card games. I also learned to play dominoes as well. I got to watch all my favorite television shows and I have seen my favorite movies as well. It has been a blast. They make me laugh in here. Plus, they all love my story and die laughing every time I tell it to them. We got to listen and watch music videos on television on Saturday and Sunday mornings, which is my absolute favorite thing to do. I really am going to miss it when I leave here. I am going to have to go back to the place where I have to be in a quiet room by myself all damn day. All I get to do, that is fun there, is bounce from wall to wall. I get to hug myself with my special jacket, but that gets boring. I want to stay here with these women and have fun. I never want to leave. Even though, I have to go back to the other place for only one more year; maybe when I leave there I will go and steal a fire truck. I may come back and get to spend more time with these women. I do not think my mom will mind. She is taking a nap in the ground, and I think she will be sleeping for a while.

Hollie

It is now a year later, and I am still stuck in this hell hole of a place. Yea, I get 3 hot meals and a bed; what kind of life can you have in jail? I am waiting on my trial to start so, a group of 12 people, can decide if I should go to jail. I am sick of things being pushed back. It was hell just waiting those 60 days for the DAs office to pick up my charges. And now that they have, I am ready to get this all over and done with. I mean yes, I do understand the severity of my case, but I was sick and very much tired when I gave my daughter cold medicine in her bottle on accident and almost killed her. My husband, well ex-husband now, came to visit me a few months ago to inform me that he had filed the divorce papers with his lawyers. He had signed the divorce papers; needed me to sign them and send them back to my attorney. He would then send them to my ex husband's lawyer as soon as possible. I must admit, I was over being pissed at him. He knew that I would never in my life try to kill our baby. We had been trying for the past 8 years of our marriage to have a baby. And even though I had a ton of miscarriages, he knew I was so excited God gave us our beautiful bundle of Joy. So, why would I try and kill her? I am so mad and disappointed in myself. I hope and pray that my attorney can work things in my favor and get me out of here. He has definitely told me to stay positive. But, he has also warned me as well. My ex-husband plans to take the stand and testify on how much of an unfit mother he thinks I am. I am not sure exactly what to do but pray at this point. I hope that these 12 people will have sympathy in their hearts for me; when they hear my story. I plan to let them know how much I love my baby. How much I adore her. How much she really means to me. I want them all to know I was a more than capable and a great mother to my beautiful daughter. She was and still is the love of my life. I would do any and everything for her. Especially if it means that I can get out of jail and be with her again.

Anita

It has been a little over 20 years since I have seen my foster brother. After I filed a report to have him investigated for my foster parents, his real parents, murder he was sentenced after a lengthy trial. He was sent to jail for 20 years, 10 years per parent. Now he has done his time and I wonder if he will even see me. He got out yesterday. I am more than sure he is going to come back to our parent's house to get some of his things. I am sitting at the kitchen table waiting for him. He walks in. I can tell from the look on his face, he is livid. He is definitely not happy to see me. The only reason I am here is to talk to him. I ask him to sit down and listen to what I have to say. I know now, since he has done time and the statue of limitations is up, I cannot be prosecuted for the same crime. So, now is a great time to get everything off my chest. I let him finally know the truth. I first tell him that he was just as wrong as our parents were, from the time when he would not tell the cops about our parents molesting us as children, when I had called them one night. So, that was the reason I framed him. First, I killed our parents and hid the bodies. Then, I took all the evidence and planted it so that it looked like he had killed them. I had even given the police the tip about where the bodies could have been, to make sure that he would be convicted. I also let him know that I am not sorry for killing them, nor I am sorry for getting him locked up. Had he protected me then, when we were kids, maybe I would have protected him 20 years ago. Maybe, he would have not gone to jail for a crime I committed.

Kate

It had been a year and a half and to my surprise, I had a parole hearing. My son had passed the bar, as soon as he did, he became my lawyer. He did any and everything in his power to be a better man than his dad. He tried so hard to get me out. When I went to court, saw my husband on the stand, and heard everything he said, I was shocked. I can tell he understands how much he has hurt me. I cannot help but think that the only reason he told the court I should get out, is all for my son and daughter. Even though I no longer love him, he does love our kids. I know he would give anything to have them back in his life. When the judge decided to let me out and also revoke the rest of my parole sentence and give me credit for time served, I knew I could start my life over. The very first thing I did, when I was released from jail, was go back to the house where I raised my children and made a home for my family. I cooked a huge meal and called my kids over. When my husband walked through the door I told him to sit down and I poured him a drink. I could see the excitement in his eyes. When our kids got there, we all ate our dinner and dessert like a happy family. I handed my husband a stack of papers and told him to sign them. His happiness turned to hurt immediately. I told him I wanted nothing from him. All I wanted was this divorce and my car; which, I had bought myself years ago when we first got married. He could tell for the first time, in so many years, I wanted to be away from him. My kids then informed him, if he did not sign the papers, they would never speak to him again. I think that did it for him. He signed, even though he did not want to. For the first time of my life, I felt free and alive. I felt like I could finally be happy. I gave the signed divorce papers to my son, kissed my husband on the cheek one last time, got in my car, and drove off smiling happily.

Rainbow (Bow)

So many years have passed and I am so thankful for my best friend. Even though the judge had sentenced me to life, in about a year I get to possibly get out on parole. And for that I am most certainly thankful. I know I was wrong for killing my pimp and the father of my son, but he definitely deserved it. But my son is safe now, he never has to worry about someone touching him again, he is a great kid though. He will be graduating from college soon. He wants to open up a shelter for kids and parents who are molested. He is such a great child. I talk about him constantly. I think that my Bunkie is very tired of hearing about him. I could care less though. She will be in the electric chair within days. She is crazy. She set up her twin to go down for something she did. How horrible is that? At least I killed someone who hurt my family. She hurt someone just for the fun of it, let her tell it. But she will get what is coming to her just like my pimp. But me, I could possibly be out in time enough to see my son walk across the stage. I missed his middle school and even his high school graduation, but I do not plan to miss the next one. I have done everything I could to make sure I can get out and my lawyer is more than confident that I will get out, so now I will have to wait and continue to be positive because I know God has my back behind my back on this.

Chanie

My baby is so freaking cute. Thank god it was not a girl. I got out of jail just before my due date and had a bouncy baby boy. He has the cutest little button nose and huge little cheeks. I want to eat him up. Now that he is talking and walking, he has become a little monster. Crazy thing is, he really does remind me of my sister so much. I hate to say it but he is more like her than me, which seems weird. But then again, I did hate her the whole time I was pregnant. She definitely was my worst enemy when I needed her the most. For that reason, I have not yet forgiven her. She almost let me go down for a murder she had committed. Thank goodness that she knew me well enough to come and take her lick. I am very sad although, to have this last visit with her. In about 36 hours she will be put in a chair and electrocuted to death. I am not only sad, but my heart hurts for her. My parents think this is the best thing for her, but she is still my twin. We are identical for God's sake. Her pain is my pain. I still cannot shake our ESP. I know how she feels right now. I feel like I need to be there for her, especially since no one else will. I guess that is why all of our family is mad I have written her, accepted her calls, and even put money on her books all this time. At the end of the day, she is still my sister; I shared everything with her. I have always protected her and been there for her; I cannot stop now. I will go see her this last time, pray with her, and hope God can have some mercy on her soul. I have done my part. I am going to forgive her like she has asked. I know now, she is sorry. I want to say I love you to her one last time before she is gone forever.

Tammy

Only remembering bits and pieces of a story is never a good sign, especially when it is the only way to get out of trouble. It is really sad when you realize that you were really messed up. So sad, you cannot remember the exact events from a night when you killed 3 people. I guess, my drinking really was a problem. Too bad I will never in my life get to drink again. I guess this life sentence is my punishment for not doing the right thing. I should have not driven home that night. Well it is not time for shoulda, coulda, wouldas now. What is done is done. The worse part of my trail, I must admit is when: the dead mom, dad, and son I killed were shown on pictures they had as evidence from the crash. The photos from the accident were the worse. I think the son who was not in the car, and his testimony, really broke me down. Knowing, he now at the age of 22, is all alone makes me feel like a horrible person. No mom, no dad, no one. Just him. I feel like the most horrible person in the world. I think it was when he took the stand, the jury made it up in their minds; I should be put away for the rest of my life. I do not blame them. I hope that when I go to meet my maker, God can have more mercy on me, than I had on the family I killed that night.

Canella

Life is like the game monopoly; I have learned. One minute you are stuck in jail and then the next minute you roll the dice, and pull the get out of jail free card. Anyone else would have used theirs, me on the other hand, I decided not to. My lawyer was shocked when I decided I wanted to do my time, instead of get out of jail and go home to celebrate my 65th birthday. I had no family and my friends I had in my twenties, had all gone on home to glory. My bunk mate, Lizzie, would say that she thought I was crazy, but she respected my decision. Not everyone could make that kind of decision. The only reason I did decide to stay in jail is because as long as I am here I am safe. I can take my chemo and radiation and have a chance to fight this cancer. But, everything is up to the man upstairs. This decision was mine. This decision was the one thing that I got to decide for myself. It was my way of having some kind of control in this hell known as jail. I guess life just sucks like that. I am still here with cancer, but I am still in my right mind; I am still making it. God is really and truly great. All that I can do is praise him. But today has been a hard day. My heart for some reason hurts. Lizzie keeps telling me everything will be okay. She even prayed for me tonight. She is really the blessing I needed. Even though she killed a cop she is a good girl and has become such a good friend. I am very happy that I could have helped her find peace in the lord. She has helped me find peace within myself. I do not feel like I can shake this pain though. I think that my maker is looking for me right now; I really need to go see what he wants. But, I think Lizzie is going to be mad at me. Looks like I am going to miss our morning prayer tomorrow. I hope she can forgive me.

Teena

I never got to see my parents face before I was sent to face the judge who told me I would be on trial for two counts of manslaughter for the murder of the twins I was babysitting, who drown. They did not come to visit me after that either. They did not even answer the phone or write me when I would try to reach out to them. I think when I lost my boyfriend that was the last straw for me. I felt like I honestly had nothing to live for anymore. I lost my family and all my friends in the matter of minutes feels like. I am not sure how any 16 year old could deal with the hand I was dealt. I guess, I could not deal with the hand either. I would never see prom or graduation. I would never get my license or my first car at 18. I would miss out on breaking my virginity and even falling in and out of love for the first time. In jail you tend to think and over think every situation and every possibility. Maybe that is the reason my next move was my last move. I never got to make it to my 17th birthday. But, there was a nice celebration in my honor, before that day came. It was a sad and rainy day out, but my parents still decided to have my funeral. Even though they sent me to jail, my neighbors had experienced the pain of losing their children. I assume that was the reason they attended my funeral. I maybe dead and gone but, I guess it was not so bad after all. Now, I get to watch their kids all the time.

Layla

I think that I have one of the worse lawyers by far. I did not get off because of him doing his job, horribly. Plus, I was made an accomplice in a murder trial I had nothing at all to do with. Boy was I mad when I got a sentence of 5 years for helping Khloe kill that drug dealer. I honestly wanted to kill her. Had I ever gotten my hands on Khloe, I would have gotten another charge I swear. But after a year, things seemed to change for the better. I do not know if it was because of guilt or because she was truly sorry for everything. Or maybe she really was my best friend still; maybe she was still the person I used to play jump rope and baby dolls with all the time. But something in Khole was still good, maybe not pure. She had confessed to everything. She told the truth. Even though it was a year later, it was better late than never at all. It is better now. I can go back to school. I can start over. Now I am happy that I get another chance at life, but for Khloe, those added years to her time will take all of her good years. I am pretty sure her family is livid, her father especially. He is that kind of man. He does not like to be made a fool of, neither does her grandfather. I hope that she will be alright. I pray she can make it. Khloe is strong as hell, me on the other hand, I will be fine for sure. I will never trust anyone like I did her ever again, that is the only down side. But I will still be a good best friend and go see her. I maybe mad but forgiveness was always something the lord said we should carry within us.

Khloe

Being sentenced to 10 years for murder is one thing, but getting 5 years for a murder you had nothing to do with was that bullshit. When I found out Layla did not turn on me, but got 5 years as well, it made me feel like shit. She was truly my best friend. Too bad I did not know how to be hers. Shit Layla was the only friend I had. She always had my back. Her getting time proved it. My dad could have passed out and died when I said I wanted to confess after the trial. He advised me not too because we had already been sentenced. H said I could probably get more time. It did not matter. Layla did not need to be in here. She did not deserve it. It took me a year to finally get the truth out. Yea, I got my time plus hers, but I felt better about myself. I will not lie; I was surprised when she came to visit me. I thought I would never see her again. As bad as I felt, I wanted her to forgive me. Her being the great friend I know she is, she finally did. I know that I would never become a lawyer like my father, but I would also never become a horrible person like him either. My peace and my sanity were the only things that matter to me. My peace of mind is all that I needed. I know will be in jail for 15 years. But doing that time, knowing my friend forgives me; will help make it better.

Cash

Lord knows I do not like a lot of people in my house. It is bad enough I have to deal with the kids all over the house all the time. My children are so damn friendly and love everyone. They definitely have Hope's glimmer. She says they are just like me, but whatever. I have to keep telling them sit the hell down somewhere. All they want to do is run all over the beach. It is usually okay, but the back yard they are used to playing in, has people all over setting up for this damn wedding. I do not know why I let Hope talk me into opening a wedding planning company and bar. She does all the weddings. I focus on the food and drinks and I run the bar; we do a pretty great job together. We have always made a hell of a team. When I got out of jail, after Hope, we moved to Hawaii and bought our home on the beach. We still had it. I think we are still a little too close for comfort. It makes me smile because she is so happy and loves our life. Today however, is the day, I can see the sparkle in her eyes and the joy on her face. She is planning her best friend's, Lillie, wedding. If it were not for Lillie, when Hope got out, I do not know if Hope would have made it. But I am thankful for Lillie. She is our silent business partner, who is not so silent. She is also the god mother of our children. It is a grand day because she is marrying my best friend. My best friend was the hall girl while we were in jail, Byrd. She and I became close in jail and even closer through our women. In jail, Byrd was the reason Hope and I could talk and help each other stay strong. When she got out, she proposed to Lillie, and asked me to be her best man. I could not say no. It only took Lillie and Hope a year to plan the perfect weeding and use our house to do it. But, I cannot wait for this wedding to be over. I am truly happy for them, none the less. I honestly hope, right now, this studzilla is dressed and ready. We do not have that much longer till the wedding starts and I know the girls will flip out if we are late. I am ready to get my best friend married; and get my house and family back to normal!

Hope

It is the first day, in a long time, I can say I am blissfully happy. Today, I am attending a wedding in my backyard on the beach. Everything is gorgeous. This has to be one of the best weddings I have ever planned, if I do say so myself. It is such a happy day for everyone. Cash's and my kids are running around like always and I can hear her yelling at them to go sit the hell down. I always laugh because they are just like her, wild and free. She and I have made such a beautiful family. We both decided on how we would have children. First, after we got married, she would have a baby. That was our oldest boy. Then, I would have a baby. That was our 2nd son. We later decided to adopt a baby. And that is how we got our bright and beautiful baby girl. They are all so different, yet they all act the same, just like Cash. Our home is a happy one. When I got out, I went and got our stash. Not too long after, Cash got out. We came to Hawaii and bought or dream home on the beach. We started a company shortly after. I planned weddings and Cash ran the bar we opened. It was the best idea we ever had. And with Lillie being our silent partner, whose voice carries, we are all doing okay. Lillie made sure I had a place to stay when I got out of jail, until Cash was released. I just stand here, and I think, it has been 6 years since we were all locked up in the same jail house together. Now I am planning Lillie and Byrd's wedding. I am so excited for them. With all she has been through, Lillie definitely deserves to be happy. I cannot wait to see her as a beautiful bride. I really cannot wait to see Byrd, now that I think about it. Her ass was a real studzilla throughout the wedding planning process. She honestly has always been somewhat of a brat, even in jail. I am very glad that she is out. I love seeing these two idiots happy. I can say that I will be glad when this whole thing is over none the less. I am ready for all these people to be gone. I am ready for Lillie and Byrd to go on their honeymoon. I am ready to have my house and my family back.

Byrd

It is finally the day I have been ready and waiting for all my life. Even though I am a stud, I still have been looking forward to my wedding day. I am so happy that after all this time I still have Lillie in my life. When I was sent to jail for 20 years, she was still there for me. She worked some kind of magic and my time was reduced. I only ended up doing 5 years. It was crazy to me how strong one woman could be. She made a friend in this woman, who I really feel was sent to us both from God, named Hope. She was the girlfriend of another woman that was in our dorm, and my best friend, Cash. These two definitely kept Lillie grounded. They showed her that fast money was not necessary. I am thankful for them helping her to maintain her legal business tender. She is a business partner with them, who I knew for damn sure was not silent. Lillie is never silent, but that is one reason I love her. I am so excited that she is going to be my wife. She will look stunning, I know it. Our wedding is on the beach, in the most beautiful backyard ever. Well its Hope and Cash's backyard. I can hear the kids running around and Cash yelling at them. It just makes me laugh. They are the cutest and best god children Lille and I could have. They definitely brighten up our day. I can hear Cash's ass coming up the stairs now. I guess it is time for me to finish getting my ass dressed and ready to stand at the end of this aisle. As cash comes in the door, I am excited because we look some damn good in our tuxes. Our women are going to be all over us tonight. As me and Cash make our way downstairs and outside, then to the end of the isle, I wait patiently for Lillie. Everyone stands up and here she comes. I am speechless when I see her in all white. My breath literally leaves my body and I am taken back by her beauty. I have never seen a woman as stunning as her. We start the ceremony, say our vows, and then we say I do. As I kiss her lips my knees shake. I know now, not only am I marrying my best friend, but also the woman of my dreams.

Lillie

After 5 years of waiting and one year of planning, I am more than excited for Byrd's and my wedding day. Thanks to Hope and Cash. They are giving me my dream wedding with my dream woman. It is a little bit corny, but I love her. I am so happy. As I finish getting my make up done, Hope comes in to help me put on my dress. I literally get butterflies in my belly and almost start crying. I do not want to ruin my make up so I immediately stop. All I can think is that I am about to marry my best friend. As I walk down the aisle, I see Byrd. I never take my eyes off her. It is like no one else is there but her and I. She really looks good in her tux. I want to pounce on her. I get to the end of the aisle. We exchange our vows. We then say those beautiful words, I do. My body is literally filled with goose bumps when we kiss. God I love this damn woman. We walk down the aisle hand in hand as everyone is throwing rose petals at us. We are so elated. We enjoy our guests and dance and eat and drink. Somewhere in the midst of one of the slow songs, we realize how lucky we both are. Our god daughter, Cash and Hope's youngest child, comes up to me and asks when we are going to have a little baby for her to play with? I laugh and look at Byrd and say, "I guess it is time." We ask for everyone's attention. We tell them that we have an announcement to make. We thank everyone for their love and support. We tell them we are grateful for them coming out to celebrate with us this great day. We look at one another and exchange a huge smile and we say at the same exact time, "We are pregnant." Everyone starts screaming and crying and congratulating us. We are so happy we embrace one another in a kiss, and forget about everyone else there.

Leslie

It has been years and I am going to be in isolation for probably a few more months before they send me back into general population. I really do hate it there. My jaw always seems to be in pain when I am in there. I guess that is from the memory of that ass whipping I got some years ago. I am so baffled by all that has happened to me. I ended up getting life without the possibility of parole, behind the woman whose head I bashed in. When she decided to sue the police department she became a millionaire. I was stuck in here, miserable. The trial I had was so crazy. Not only were DA agents and police officers taking the stand against me, they were all people who I knew and had worked with. It seemed like all my enemies were on her side. She was one hell of a woman. She was smart and crafty and had a hell of a lot of people on her payroll. She was the one woman I feared the most. She took my life away, but she got to start a new one for herself. I have definitely learned the meaning of the phrase 'Bad Bitch.' She was someone I know I could never forget. I came to find out she was definitely well known among many people within the law enforcement agencies. I hope our paths never cross again. I want to do my time in peace. No more fights. No more conflicts. I have come to the point where my thoughts and memories of the outside world are all I have. I will keep those, my faith, and my prayers with God. That way, I can make it in jail, one day at a time.

Epilogue

8 months and 12 days later

When I get the call that Lillie is going into labor, I rush myself to the hospital. I come down the hall and I can hear screaming. I know it is Lillie. I can tell she is in a lot of pain. When I open the door to her hospital room, I see Hope with this look of anguish in her face. She was squinting. Lillie is squeezing the life out of her hand. I look over at the recliner chair on the other side of the room and see Cash. She looks like she is about to pass out. I touch Hope on the shoulder and force Lillie's hand from around hers. I guide Hope toward Cash, who looks like she needs her. I look at Lillie; I tell her I am here now and everything will be okay. I tell her to breathe and try to take it easy. She starts to calm down and focus. About 17 hours and maybe a million pushes later, our little bundle is here. We are captivated by her beauty. With eyes like her mother, she is so gorgeous. Lalani is her name and beauty is wrapped all around her. Lillie is laying there more beautiful than ever, caressing our baby girl's head. She bends down and kisses the baby's forehead ever so softly. I cannot help but be proud of her. She looks up at me and whispers, "Byrd we did it." In that moment the tears fall from my face and I smile at my beautiful wife and daughter.